MAN
OR
Angel

Tina Rosemary Ojukwu

authorHOUSE®

AuthorHouse™ UK
1663 Liberty Drive
Bloomington, IN 47403 USA
www.authorhouse.co.uk
Phone: UK TFN: 0800 0148641 (Toll Free inside the UK)
UK Local: 02036 956322 (+44 20 3695 6322 from outside the UK)

Published by AuthorHouse 06/12/2020

ISBN: 978-1-7283-5385-2 (sc)
ISBN: 978-1-7283-5386-9 (e)

Print information available on the last page.

Any people depicted in stock imagery provided by Getty Images are models, and such images are being used for illustrative purposes only. Certain stock imagery © Getty Images.

Scriptures marked KJV are taken from the KING JAMES VERSION (KJV): KING JAMES VERSION, public domain.

Scriptures marked NKJV are taken from the NEW KING JAMES VERSION (NKJV): Scripture taken from the NEW KING JAMES VERSION®. Copyright© 1982 by Thomas Nelson, Inc. Used by permission. All rights reserved.

This book is printed on acid-free paper.

God said, let us make man in our own image, after our likeness. Let him have dominion over the earth, over the animals, the seas9Gen.1:26).

Angels were created from the beginning by God and they are not creators with God.

Let the Angels praise the Lord as they were created to praise him (Psalm 148:2,5).

This demonstrates how special we are compared with Angels. The word of God said, don't know, you are gods and co-heads with him. We as human kind will judge Angels.

Humanity was not made in the image of Angels but rather in the image of God. When God created humankind, He made them in the likeness of God.

Male and female, he created, blessed them and named them humankind (Gen 1:5).

Creation belongs to the will of God and not man.

God did not make the decisions with the counsel of Angels.

God states the men are like us (Gen3:2)

At tower of babel, God went and confused their language and scatter humankind on face of the earth (Gen 11:7).

Angels were created to serve mankind and those who received them were blessed (Gen.32:26). Angels were created for their purpose (Gen.18:9). They are not ghost or departed human beings. Angels have been in existence just like other things created before God created human beings on this planet earth. When God created spirits, He created Angels out of nothing as opposed to us created in the image of God. He then created human and said let us make man in the image of God and likeness of God. Let them have dominion over the fish of the sea, cattle on the earth and over every living, moving creature (Gen. 1:26). This is why the scripture said who is man that thou at mindful of him and the son of man that thou visited; behold you have made him a little bit lower than the Angels (Prov. 8:22).

He visits us always with his Angels watching over all that concerns us. This illustrates that even though God has placed mankind lower than the Angels, yet His counsel and purpose is that Angels should serve mankind. We are seated in the heavenly places far above principalities, powers and spiritual wickedness in the high places. The Angels are not seated like us. We are referred to as the gods, sons of God, joint head with Christ, heirs of salvation which the angels are not (Heb.1:14). Anything created by God should not be worshipped, so Angels worship us, pets and animals listen to us, so do angels listen to our command to go to war on our behalf. Angels were created to minister to us and cause us to be at peace (2Thessa 1:7). Angels are sexless and do not propagate or reproduce like human beings and are not given into marriage like human beings. They are immortal and not subject to death and so are we immortal if we accept Christ as savior.

Angels may resort to take up or assume human forms at times in their service to mankind. These Angels are rooted in our poetry, paintings, sculptor, and prayers. We prayed them to take over the biddings, counsel of God, to go places we cannot go.

Angels are in different categories, ranks: The Angel of the Lord distinguished from other Angels. He is the Angel of the Lord of Hosts of all Angels, he is called the face of God, and his face is the character and nature of God. It has power to pardon, retain transgressions; has power of the name of God. This Angel is God himself (Ex33:14). He is called Angel of his presence, to be our ever present help in trouble and in times of needs. This Angel of God is uncreated. The Arch Angel is the chief Angel and carry messages of highest importance. They care of principalities of nations on our behalf and have high icu. Angels run countries, deal with precepts, education, systems, media that concerns us. They rule in the affairs of men and turn their hearts to suit his people. Demonic powers work with principles (Col2; Eph2:23; 6:7). These Angels are called the Cherubim, have retributions and redeeming powers, projections (Gen 3:24; Ex22:25). They have face of lions, and have characters of eagles. They represent intelligence and have ability to make decisions. Even with all these attributes, Angels were created to serve mankind. King David in the scriptures referred to King Saul and Jonathan as swifter than the eagles as and stronger than the lions, so God wants us to see ourselves as greater than the characteristics of Angels. Angel Michael was the guiding

Angel of the Israelites and the church. Behold I sent an Angel before thee to keep thee in all thy ways and to bring you into the prepared place (Ex3:14; 20:23). God said, my Angels will go ahead of you to bring you into the land of Amorites, Hittites, Kenites, Kenizzites Kadmonites, Perizzites, Rephaims, Girgashites Jebusites, Hivites, Cananites and God wiped off the enemies. The commandments were made conditional if they obey the Angels to guide them through it. The Angels of God travelling in front of the Israelites army then withdrew and went behind them, which explains the guiding Angel can be before, behind, left and right hand side. The pillar of cloud also went from front to behind. Angels guide us from geographical errors and bad conducts. They are enemies to our enemies and adversaries to our adversaries. The Angels watch over us as spirits beings. God will cause Angels to fulfill the number of days in our lives. Angels appeared to Abraham and made a covenant unto his seed Gen 15:18-21). The Angel provided water for Hagar and Ishmael. The Lord said to Joshua, I have given you Jericho (Jos 6:2). An Angel provided food for Elijah (1kgs 19:5-24). God opened Gehazi's eyes, Elisha's servant to see horses and chariots of Angels when he was afraid they might be defeated. Daniel prayed and caused the warrior angel to go into actions for him (Dan 3:2). There are things in life we cannot control or guide against, Angels do this for us and impacts our lives. Angels identify with the second person of the trinity to keep us in his way as we go through the wilderness of life (Matt 1:20). The messenger angels carry out the purposes of God. They are heavenly host with incredible strength, supernatural knowledge. They know all things but yet they serve mankind. What an incredible God with ultimate love for us. He has put Angels with all this title and responsibilities to serve us. What an amazing, awesome God, worthy of our praise and worship. They carry out God's assignments and execute God's words. They make every word of God happen and do his pleasures. The Angels bring us into the prepared place which God has for us (Ex23:20). They trample on the evil works of the enemy on our behalf (Psalm35:5; 91). They defend us in battle, the Angel smooth Balaam trying to curse Israel (Num22:24). The Angel built a hedge around Job so that the enemy could not touch him (Job 1:10). When the enemy rises up like a flood, the standard of God's Angels silences them. (Psalm 34:7). He is our Jehovah Rohi that sent his angelic prophet to deliver Daniel from the lion's Den (Dan10:13). Angels sent to Gedion to affirm his place in God as mighty man of valour (Judg6:11). The Angel delivered Peter out of the prison (Acts12:7-8). Angels builds a hedge around us like Job to stop how far Satan can go (Job1:10) Angels are assigned to get us to our destinations and bring answers to prayers. Angels warns of God's justice and judgments (Jude1:7). One Angel killed Pharaoh, took care of Lucifer and the Dragon (2Peter2:11; Ps103:11). Angels that fought the dragon was mentioned in (Rev4:6; 7:1) and variety of Angels in (Rev15) and the seven Angels with plagues. Angels announced the message of the birth of Jesus to the Shepherds and minister to Christ after the temptations in the desert and proclaimed his resurrection from the death (Luk2:14). One Angel rolled away the stone and strengthened our savior in his agony on the cross. Mary was told by an Angel Christ is risen on the resurrection day. An Angel redeemed Magdalene from evil spirit. Angels appeared to Lot before destruction of Sodom and Gomorrah, warning of coming destruction (Gen19). One Angel destroyed 85,000 men in Assyrian camp on behalf of the Israelites. God sent an Angel to John to write the seven churches. Angels releases healing virtues, fights sicknesses. Angel asked the question to Prophet Ezekiel can these bones live and Ezekiel answered if you say so (Ez37). Angels reveals things which must come to pass (Rev22:6-8). Angels carry songs of conquests and John worshipped at the feet of Angel that showed end times. Angels guided Rebekah's marriage to Isaac from the clan of Abraham (Gen24:40). Jacob was met on his way to Mahanaim by Angel of the Lord (Ps34:7).

Man will judge Angels (1Cor6:1-3; Heb2:1-8). Angels are human messengers and nowhere did Angels rule or sit on the throne (Rev 1:3). Angels played a prominent role in the apocalypses mentioned sixty-six times, the cloud, rainbow and the sun. I saw the Angel who stand by before God and to them were given 7 trumpets (Rev 8:1). Letters were written to Angels in Rev 2-3, 14). Angels sang when he had taken the scroll (Rev5:8-11

Angels were the very first of God's creation (2Cor 4:14). They are inferior to the supreme God (Col 1:16). Angels are evidently ministers of God, and there was war in Heaven and Angel Michael and his Angels fought the dragon, one of the Angel with seven vials (Rev 17:1-18).

God created the Angels before He created the universe and the Angels were mentioned in conjunction with Satan (Matt 25:24).

The unique thing that God did was about forming man. He formed man from the dust of the earth that he created. He formed us the content and on the day of Pentecost, the content was blown into container to contain the spirit. God is a former, He formed the things and fills it. He formed man and filled him with the breath of God. Every breath we take is his breath. He is a porter on the wheel, we are the vessel of clays. Before I formed you in your mother's womb, I knew you (Jer 1:7). On the sixth day God formed man. Man was the only creature God touched and we have been needy to be touched by God, by wants, needs, hunger, tastes. The Bible is our best source of knowledge about Angels (Ps 91:11; Matt 18:10; Acts 12:15). Angel of the Lord spoke to Philip, arise and go to the desert (Acts 8:26). The illusions of Angels Col 2:15, 1kgs 11:2; Ez9:14; 2Cor6:14-18; Acts 7:53). Satan masqueraded as an Angel of light (Matt25:41;2Cor 11:13-14 Angels are mentioned 108 times in the old Testament and 165 times in the new testament.

I will be looking through the book of the bible to see where angels are mentioned and their roles and positions compared with man. The Doctrines of Angels, their analysis compare to human beings.

Angels were mentioned 59 times out of the 66 books of the Bible. They were mentioned 108 times in Old Testament and 165 times in the New Testament. The ruling Angels are mentioned in (Eph 3:10). There are 227 references to Angels in Old Testament (Gen 1:19; Ep1:5-12). He God was seen by Angels and announces then to the nations of the world, the good works coming. These doctrines must be shown forth by fruits of the spirit (1Thi 3:6; 6:11; 1Jh 5:21). The mystery of godliness, which God was in the flesh, talked about army of angels (Jos 10:12; 1Th 4:13; 2Thi 1:18). The Angels elect reminds God's people of things (2Thi 1:5; 4:1). The Angels are before lowly in the eyes of men (1 Cor1:27, 3:18-20; 4:9). Know ye not ye shall judge Angels (Eph1:21). We are sitted in Heavenly places far above principalities, powers with might dominion over every name that is named in this world and the world to come. Angels are God's male men (1Th 4:6; Rev 12:7). The Lord with his Angels in flaming fire (2Th 1:7; 1Peter2:11). Seven Angels mentioned with seven trumpets (Is 27:13, Matt 24:29-31). Innumerable company of Angels were mentioned in (Gen2:1; Ps 68:17; Dan 7:10; Matt 26:53 and Heb 13:2). Be not forgetful to entertain strangers for thereby you entertain Angels unaware. They are ministering Angels sent to minister to them who shall be heirs of salvation (Ps 148; Isai 40:26; Luk 1:26;-38; Heb 1:4 Rev 21:9-10). Paul mentioned five separate powers already present in (1Cor 15:24; Rom 8:38;2Thi 1:7) Herod was suddenly killed by an Angel for arrogating himself honour due God (Acts 5:17; 14:14;16:19). A vision that appeared to Paul at night stood a man of

Macedonia, an Angel in the form of a man. Paul reference to tongues of Angels (1Cor 13:1; Lev21:17-23)). Angel Gabriel appeared to prophet Zechariah and Virgin Mary foretelling the birth of John (Luk 1:20-38; 20:36). In the sixth month of Elizabeth's pregnancy, God sent Angel Gabriel. Angel release Paul and Silas from prison (Acts 1:10). An Angel freed Peter from King Herod, tapped him on the side to get up and Peter went to the house of Mary (Acts 12:3-12). The Angels also are living witnesses to us (1 Thi1:8; 6:13-20; 2Thi 1:14-22;3:8;4:4). God sent Angels living and dead were quoted also in (Rom 14:10; Is 45:23). Angels were in (Gen 6:38). Philip wrote about Angels and demons, talked about protection of guardian Angels (Heb12:22). The Angel mentioned in the spiritual warfares (Eph 6:10). There was a violent Earthquake for an Angel (Matt 1:20-22). Angels were divided into ranks, orders. The Angel announced the birth of Jesus to the shepherds. Angels are mentioned again in Jesus temptations, Satan is the chief enemy of the gospel (Matt4:11; 13:19). The Bible is our best source of knowledge about Angels (Psalm 91:11; Matt18:10; Acts12:10). Angel of the Lord spoke to Philip to arise and go to the desert (Acts 8:26). The book of Enoch mention Angel's 200times reports about Angels. Angels have been in existence just like other things created by God before we showed up on this planet earth. Angels been with us for centuries rooted in poets, painters, sculptors, prayers. Emphatically, Angels are around us with his images on ornaments, cards, clothes etc. Angels resort or take up human forms or personality at times. In some instances, Angel of the Lord is a theophany an appearance of God in the physical form. The Angel of the Lord are never mentioned in the New Testament after the birth of Christ. Those who received Angel's messages are blessed (Gen32:26). When God created Spirits, He created Angel for their purpose (Ex 20:16, Gen 16:9).

Gen1:1 In the beginning God created the heaven and the earth and angels were created. And in Gen. 1:26 and said let us make man in our own image, after our likeness: and let them have dominion over the fish of sea, and over the cattle, and over all the earth, and over every creeping thing that creepeth upon the earth.

We see in this chapter of the book of Genesis that God gave man dominion over the earth and such dominion was not giving to angels.

Further, in Gen 1:27 God created man in his own image, in the image of God created he him; male and female created he them. This was not the case with angel, not created from the image of God.

Angels were created to minister to us, cause us to be at peace (2The 1:7) from the characteristics of Angels they are creatures called out of nothing as opposed to us created in the image of God. The scripture said don't you know ye are gods. We are seated in the heavenly places far above principalities, powers, spiritual wickedness in the high places, but the angels are not seated like us in the Heavenly places.

The scripture bears us witness that as many as believe are the Sons of God and joint head with Christ. We are referred to as sons of God, which the angels are not. Any created by God should not be worshiped by us, they worship us, so do angels not created in the likeness of God. God is self existing and angels are created for a purpose. Angels are not ghost or departed human spirits (2Peter1:10-11). Angels were noticeably absent in the book of Ruth, Nehemiah, Esther (1Peter 1:9-12; 3:22). 1/3 of innumerable company of Angels choose to rebel with fallen Angels (Heb12:22).

Angels are not humans, they are spirits, not limited by physical nature, has power to assume human forms to sensually appreciate them. In order to appear to sense of man angels took human forms, and resort to human personality (Heb1:26, Psalm104:11). Angels are not male or female, has no gender, they are sexless, they do not propagate or reproduce and are not given to marriage (Luke). They are immortal and not subject to death, but humans that sin and refuses to repent and accept Christ will die and not be immortal.

Hell is a place where such spirits go and abound when the end comes. God will bound them with chains that cannot be broken.

Angels have various ranks and positions (1Peter 3:27). 1st rank, is the Angel of the Lord, distinguish from other Angels. He is called the face of God. His face is character and nature of God. It has power to pardon, retain transgressions, has power of the name of God (Exodus 33:14). He is called Angel of His presence. Angel of God is uncreated (Gen 32:48). And Joshua got instructions from Angel of the Lord. The Arch Angel is the chief Angel (Jude1:19). Arch Angels are powerful, carry messages of highest importance. They take care of principalities of nations, have high icu with lower angels. Angels run countries, deal with precepts, education systems, media What is filled with principles are at trend of demonic powers (Col.2, Eph 2:23; 6:7). Demonic powers works by principles. These Angels are called the Cherubim, have retributions and redeeming powers (Gen 3:24). They are projections (Ex 22:25). They have face of lions, eagles, their characters. They represent intelligence. These Angel represent intelligence, has ability to make decisions, can see with character of an eagle. Even with all these attributes, angels are created to serve God and his children.

The woman came and told her husband saying, a man of God came unto me and his countenance was like the countenance of an Angel of God very terrible but I asked him not whence he (was) neither told he me his name (Judg 13:6). Then Manoah realizes that it was the angel of the Lord (1sam 29:10). Angel mentioned in 2sam, jos10:13, 2sam 1:8, 2Thi 3:8. In the exilic period, Deuteronomy to Isaiah does not mention angels. The army of Senacherib is destroyed by the angel of the (Ez11:39, 2kgs 19:35). Elisha prayed for his eyes to be opened (2kgs 6:17). The seven angels are Michael, Gabriel, Raphael, the book of Daniel is followed by the Prophet, Hosea, the first of the mentioned biblical figures in a row as men of righteousness such as Noah, Daniel and Job but they are not angels. Satan rose up against Israel, God sent a plague against it. Angel called the Lord Jesus, lion of the tribe of Judah. Then Micah said hear ye the word of the Lord, the Lord is the leader of the armies of angels. Angels transcribed the prophecies of Ezra.

In 2Samuel David referred to King Saul and Jonathan as swifter than the eagles and as stronger than the lions. God wants us to rise beyond the eagles characteristics, do his biddings and to trust us with holiness. Isaiah 6, talks about Seraphim with most burning love for God. It has 9 wings and comes from alter of God's fire.

There are things in life we cannot control and guide against, angels guides and impacts our lives.

Angel Michael was the guardian Angel of the Israelites and the Church. Daniel prayed and cause Angel Gabriel to go into actions for him. Daniel experienced Angelic visitation (Dan 3:2). Witness in Spirit makes moment better. Behold I sent an Angel before thee to keep thee in all thy ways and to bring you into the place, I prepared for you (Exd 3:14, 20, 23). So far we see Angel's servitude to God and man. The book of Isaiah mentioned the Seraphim with six wings. Isaiah vision of the Lord in his glory (Isa 42:19; Malachi 3:10). The Angel that ascended above the heights of the clouds and to be like the most high was cast down (Isa14:14). In the book of Ezekiel Angel Gabriel was sent to destroy Jerusalem in chariots of fire (

Angels are spirits, flames of fire (Psalm 104:4); Blessed be ye the Lord his angels that excel in strength, that do his commandments (Psalm 103:20). He shall give his angels charge over us to keep us in all our ways (Psalm 91:11). Only fools tread where angels fear to tread. The rash or inexperienced will attempt things that wiser people are more cautious of. He said behold, I sent an Angel unto a city of Galilee named Nazareth (Matt2:13).

And Angel of the Lord spoke to Philip saying arise and go toward (Acts 8:26). The Angel Gabriel was from God unto a city of Galilee named Nazareth preached the gospel with Holy Ghost, not only for current time but also for that which is to come. It is mentioned in the book of Zechariah where Joshua was standing before the Angel of the Lord against Satan in Mt. Sinai also mentioned in Exodus. The Angel appeared to Joshua the high priest in a dream, appeared to Zechariah in a dream at Persian court, shown four horns and the mention of adversary on the right hand side (Psalm 109:6).

Angels are living proof that life is bigger than what we see. Angels warns of God's justice and judgments (Jude1:7). No matter where we go we are with angels and the glory of God. The human guardian Angels, one of the most quoted and traditionally cited as biblical evidence of Guardian Angels are mentioned in (Matt 18:10; Acts 12:15). Angel visited Joseph in a dream, not to send Mary away that the child conceived of the Holy Spirit (Matt 1:20). And the Angel answered and said unto the woman, fear not for I know that ye seek Jesus which was crucified. He is not here: for he is risen as savior, come and see the place where the Lord layed. And He shall send his Angels with great sound of trumpet mouth, the Angel Gabriel sent to Galilee named Nazareth

(Matt 24:31). Angels helped Jesus (Matt 4:11; Mar 1:13; Luk22:42). Those who do not obey gospel (Matt13:41; 49;2The1:8). See that you do not despise any of these little ones.

Angels are numerous and there are so many of them everywhere Daniel 5:10). (Heb 2:32, 12:22 He is the Lord of Hosts of all Angels.

The book of Haggai went where Angels fail to tread.

Sometimes Angels are described as celestial beings, hellonistic. Revelation talks about guardian Angels watching over his people (Rev 4:6).

Angels being greater in strength and power do not blaspheme judgment (Dan 12). Angels are explicitly mentioned twice in in (2Peter10:12, Jude 1:6, Luk20:36). The pool at Bathesida where multitude of the infirm lay, water was stirred up by an Angel (Jh 1:5). The two Angels in white were seen by Zechariah and he went mute (Jh 20:12). The same Angel told Mary, they had taken away her Lord (Jh 20:2).

Angels have greater wisdom than men (2Sam).

James talked about how the Angel of Satan existed and must be resisted (1Peter5:8). The book of Peter talked about how the Angels would like very much to know about the things we were told (1Peter1:12). It was revealed that their services was not to themselves but to us.

Angels were cast down from all their glory and dignity into chains of darkness (2 Peter 2:4).

Charles Spurgeon talked about how in the doctrine of election, yet God gave us redemption in place of Angels and did not cast us out of repentance.

So far we see Angel's servitude to God and man and that life is bigger than what we see that Angels guides against.

Duties of Angels.

1. Angel makes the word of God effective in our lives

2. Ministries of Angels prepares the way

3. They are released into circumstances and they nudge us

4. Angels are our defense in times of trouble; they give us aid (Heb 2:16) Is what God do for man and does not do for the Angel.

5. Angels builds a hedge around us to stop the Satan on how far he goes (Job 1:10).

6. Angels delivers us from the lion's Dens as the case of Daniel and when we don't realize we are stronger than lions through the power of God that works in us to will and to do his good pleasure.

7. Angels release healing virtues, book of Ezekiel, 37, made dried bones to live in the valley of dried bones.

8. Angels are assigned to get us to our destinations and bring answers to prayers.

9. Angels sent to Gideon to keep him in the book of Judges.

10. One Angel can destroy the work of Hell in our live.

11. One Angel killed Pharaoh. And one Angel smooth the first born of Egypt layed hold on Dragon 2 Peter 2:11; Psalm 103:11. They excel in strength. Two Angels appeared at the tomb of resurrection of Jesus Christ (2Jh 20:2).

12. One Angel took care of Lucifer

13. One Angel roll away the stone

14. One Angel destroyed 85,000 men in Assyrian camp, Just to mention some.

15. In Exodus Angels are referred to as Elohim. In the book of lamentation it was a consuming angel (1:12; 4:7).

16. In Daniel Angels minister salvation, about coming of Christ by Angel Gabriel (Dan 4:16) Angels are our heavenly guide (Dan 8:16).

In the book of Hosea, talks about God's followers (Hosea1:10). He struggled with the angel and overcame him, he wept, as if the angel wept and supplicated (Hosea 12:2; 32:24).

In the book of Amos, Amos had his dream about angels descending and ascending mentioned in Edom (Amos (1:11). Prophet Amos mentioned how the angels poured out his vial into the air, as doom. The angel cried holy, holy is the Lord of hosts (Amos 5:22).

In the book of Jonah, the angel commanded him to preach to Nineveh, to capture Nineveh by order of the angel before God destroyed it by prophecy.

You have Nephili where angels are referred to as the sons of God

17. In the book of Luke, the Angels strengthened the Saviour in his dying agony on the cross.

   In the book of Malachi, he is referred as Jehovah Sabbath, the Lord of hosts promised (Mala 3:1).

18. God sent an Angel to John to write to seven churches.

19. Angels have the power to make the word of God effective in our lives. Moses pleaded with the Angel of the Lord in the burning bush in the book of Exodus for his presence to go with Him, Always so he can find rest.

20. Angels acts as our defense militarily during troubles.

21. Angels builds a hedge around us to stop Satan on how far he goes or can go (Job 1:10).

22. Angels releases healing virtues, fights the sicknesses (Ezk 37). Angels asked the question can these bones live? Ezekiel answered if u say so (Ezekiel 40).

23. Angels brings answers to our problems or circumstances.

24. Angels assigned to Gideon in the book of Judges to tell him to walk as might man of valour, not to think himself as nothing.

25. Angels reveals things which must come to pass (Rev 22:6-8).

26. Angel carry songs of conquests.

27. John worshipped at the feet of the Angel that showed end times.

28. Angel guided Rebekah's marriage from the clan of Abraham to Isaac (Gen 24:40; 32).

29. Jacob went on his way and Angel of the Lord met him on his way to Mahanaim (Psalm 34:7).

30. Angel redeemed Magdalene from evil.

31. Mary was told by Angel that Christ is risen on the resurrection day.

32. Angels announced the birth of Jesus to the Shepherd (Luke 2:14) minister to Christ after the temptations in the desert and during his agony on the cross and proclaim his resurrection from the dead (Luke Matt 4:11; 24:31; Luke 22:43; John 20:12).

Jesus Christ stated the Angels of little ones continuously behold the face of the Father (Matt 18:10) this passage has been traditionally cited as biblical evidence of Guardian Angel.

33. Angels will come with Christ on the day judgement (24:31), and the Angel will separate the wicked from the just on the last day (Matt 13:49). Although the Angels do not know the day of judgement (Matt 13:32).

34. God sent an Angel to free apostle Paul in the prison, jailed by King Herod (Acts 2:7-11). (Luke 20:34) God sent an Angel to free apostle Peter after he was jailed by King Herod (Acts 12:7-11).

35. Angels do God's will Psalm 103:20 (Matt 26:53) God stationed Cherubim to protect the Garden of Eden after the fall of Adam and Eve in (Gen. 3:2). God sent an Angel to punish King David and Israelites but stopped the Angel after king David repented from destroying ("Sam 24).

In the book of Joel, the angel swung his sickle on the earth gathered its grapes and threw them into the great winepress (Joel 3:2). Joel contemplated this with the angel of the Lord (Joel 1:1). The prophesy in the book of Joel followed the basic sequence of events in autumn feast (Zec3:1; 14:1). Care that we don't sentimentalize or fictionalize angelic reality.

An Angel rescued the High Priest Joshua in Zechariah.

36. Angels appeared to Lot before destruction of Sodom and Gomorrah (Gen 19) or Raphael appearing in human form to Tobias.

37. Angel which redeemed from all evils (Gen 48:16).

God will cause Angels to fulfil the number of days in our lives.

We know Angels serve man, helped prosper Abraham's servant (Gen21:17-19. The Angel helped provide water for Hagar and Ishmael; redeemed Jacob from all evils (Gen46:16).

In the book of Jude, angels are mentioned (Jude 1:6).

In Islam, angel Raphael is the fourth angel mentioned.

CATEGORIES OF ANGELS

In Revelation (8:1-2) the seven Angels stood before God with seven trumpets.

The first Angel the Arch Angel we understood poured fury on the earth. When war broke out in Heaven Michael and his Angels battled against the dragon. The dragon and his angels fought back and they were thrown down to the earth. Angel Michael described as prince of the heavenly hosts appeared 3times in the book of Daniel (Dan 8:16; 9:21) made annunciation to Mary that she would be mother of Jesus the Lord. The highest hierarchy of Angels are next to God Seraphim (Is 6:2) Cherubim (Gen 3:2; Ezekiel 10:1_22 and the throne Col, 1:16). The Cherubim has a fiery revolving sword to guard the way to tree of life after Adam's fall (Gen 3:23). The second on sea and all living things died. The third on rivers, fountains and they become blood. The Angels on water purged God's righteousness, provoked that God needs righteous people. The fourth Angel clawed their tongues full of darkness. The sixth Angel poured their vile on river Euphrates and it dried up. Among the seven, Michael, Gabriel, Raphael; Raguel;,Remies; Saragael; Uriel named in Enoch 20:1-8) asked for in the dead sea scrolls and in the Bible of the oriental Orthodox Church of Ethiopia.

We now know that Angels are watching over us all the time, step by step to our final destination. The Bible is our best source of knowledge about angels (Ps 91:11; Matt18:10; Acts 12:15) indicates humans have guardian angels.

Looking at the book of Exodus (23:20) God said to Moses, I send an Angel before you to guard you on your way. God promised to strike terror into their enemies and subject them to other scourges. Terror and dread fell on them by the power of His hand until the Israelites pass by (Ex23:23). He promised that he will drive out their enemies little by little and not ceasing until He God has destroyed them. God said, my Angels will go ahead of you bring you into the land of Amorites; Hittites; Jebusites; Hivites; Canaanites; and how God wiped them out. Angel of the covenant fulfilled this promise. We are aware of how God destroyed the enemies of Israel. God gave them the entire country, from the Red sea and the Mediterranean, the Deserts, the Euphrates on the other side (Ex23:31). God promised to bless their sustenance, avert sickness from them; cause them to multiply and prolong their days on earth. The commandments were made conditional if they obey the Angels to guide them through it and reciprocity was established. Exodus 33:2&14) and I will send an Angel before you to drive out the Canaanites.

(Joshua 3:10) this is how you will know things (Ex 14:19) the Angel of God travelling in front of the Israelites army withdrew and went behind them which explains the guiding Angel can be before, behind, one left or right hand side. The pillar of cloud also went from front and went behind them.

Angel of the Lord stood in Red to oppose Balaam riding on his donkey and his two servants with him to cause the people of God.

The living God is among you. He will surely drive out the Canaanites, Jebusite; Perizites; Amorites; Hivites; Hittites; and the Girshites.

None of the promises were absolute but the sent of Angels were absolute. Angel identify with the second person of the Trinity to keep us in his way as we go through the wilderness of life. The Angels does not guide us and prevent us from geographical errors if we fail to be guided. Angels guides us from falling into any kind of wrong conduct.

In (Ex 14:19) the Angel of God travelling in front of the Israelites army withdrew and went behind them which explains the guiding Angel can be before, behind, one left or right hand side. The pillar of cloud also went from front and went behind them.

Angel of the Lord stood in Red to oppose Balaam riding on his donkey and his two servants with him to cause the people of God.

Only one Angel wipe out Senacherib (2Sam 24:16; 2kgs 19:35). The laws were also given to Angels to fight principalities, powers and spiritual wickedness in high places (Gal 5:10; Rom 8:38; Is 40:26; Ep3:9; Psalm 33:6;Rev10:6;Col 1:16 and Ep1:21).

WHAT NOT TO DO
TO THE ANGEL.

We should not expect Angels to appear by feelings, intuition, and premonition (Jer14:14; 23:16-31; Prov28:26). Not everyone sees the Angel when they appear (Jh12:29; 2kgs6:127; Heb13:2).

We are to beware of Angels and obey his voice so we don't miss our Angels of good tidings.

We should not provoke an Angel for Angel will not pardon.

Angels are enemies to our enemies, adversary to our adversaries.

Inspite of all this, God will put us above thee Angels, God ordained the stars and moon and caused man to have dominion over it (Psalm 8:3).

U can command it to stand still at the magnitude of it. God gave us dominion over the seas, things in it but not to the Angels. We existed in God's dna before the creation. God caused man to dwell in a place little bit lower than the Angels so the Angels can serve man by reaching out to us (Prov 8:22). They watch over us as spirit beings. Angels are spiritual beings who influence mankind by illuminating one's mind with an idea, quoting scriptures. They do not predict the future (Gal 1:6-9). They do not know the future (Matt24:36; Mark 13:32). They do not know the mind of God (Rom11:34). They cannot taste death for anyone (Heb2:6-11). They did not know where Christ did die but witness his ascension (1Peter 1:10-11). They were unable to establish peace in the Heavenly places (Col1:20). They were unable to reveal truth to Heavenly places in the way that the church can in judgement (Ep3:9-10).

*In the book of Genesis, three Angels appeared to Abraham, and God appeared to him by oaks tree as he sat at the door of his tent in the heat of the day. God made a covenant with Abraham in (Gen. 15:18). He lifted up his eyes, three men stood in front of him. He ran from the tent door to meet them and bowed himself to the earth and said I have find favour in your sight. God Do not pass by your servant (Gen 18:1-3). Angel find Isaac's wife. Jacob went from Beersheba to Haran, he tarried there all night because the sun was set, saw the Angel of God ascending and descending (Gen 28:10). The Angel which redeemed me from all evil, bless the lord (Gen. 48:16). In the book of Ecclesiastes Jacob did wrestle with the Angel. Two Angels were sent to destroy Sodom but an Angel reached Lot before the flood. (Gen.19:1-13). When we cried to the Lord He heard our voice and sent an Angel (Numb. 20:16). Joshua by the Jericho wall, cried for Lord and He sent an Angel (Jos. 5:13). The Lord said, see, I have given into your hand Jericho (Jos. 6:2). The Angels ascended in the flame of (Judge 13:20) The Angel his presence saved them from afflictions in his love in the midst of a burning bush (Isa 63:9).

In Matthew An Angel appeared to Joseph the carpenter in a dream not to send Mary with child full of grace away for the Lord is with her (Matt 1:18-21). Angel appeared in a dream (Matt 2:13). Take heed that ye despise not one of these little ones; for I say unto you that in heaven their Angels do always behold the face of my father which is heaven (Matt17:3;18:10).

When the son of man shall come in His glory and all the holy Angels with Him and then shall He sit upon the throne of his glory (Matt25:31). He shall send his Angel with great sound of trumpet and they will gather together His elect from the four winds from end of Heaven to the other (Matt24:31). Zachariah was made mute (Luk1:19).

Further in the sixth month, Angel Gabriel was sent from God to a town of Galilee called Nazareth to a virgin betrothed to Joseph of the house of David as a visitor (Luke 1:26-28).

In the book of John Mary was told by an angel that Christ has risen.

In the book of Acts, Peter was rescued from the prison by an Angel who swung the prison door open in a vision (Acts 10:3).

*In the book of Exodus God sent an Angel to lead Moses, behold, I sent an Angel before you to guard you on the way and to bring you to the place which I have prepared for you. Give heed to him and hearken to his voice. Do not rebel against him, for he will not pardon transgressions (Ex23:20). The Angel of God encamps with them and delivers them who fear God (Psalm 34). God sent Angels to guard us in all our ways.

In the book of Judges, the Angels of the Lord appeared frequently and gave Samson's name. Also to Gideon to let him know he is a mighty man of valour. The appearance of Angels of the Lord ceased at the incarnation of Christ. Angels transcribed the prophecies of Ezra.

In (Psalm 103:20) Bless the Lord ye his Angels that excel in strength, that do his commandments, hearken unto the voice of his word. In the book of (Psalms 103:20) bless the Lord ye his Angels that excel in strength, that do his commandments; hearken unto the voice of his word. For He shall give His Angels charge over us to keep us in all his ways (Psa. 91:11). The Angel of the Lord encampeth around them that fear him and deliver them (Psm 34:7).

In (Isaiah 6:2) said above stood the Angel Seraphim, each Angel had six wings with twain it covered it face and with twain they fly.

In book of Daniel God sent an Angel to shut the lion's mouth and have not ate him, said Daniel to the king. Daniel said because he Daniel was found blameless. In all their distress, He too was distressed and the Angel of his presence saved them; In his love and mercy, He redeemed them; He lifted them up, and carried them all the days of old (Isiah 63:9).

The book of Obadiah is the shortest book in the Old Testament. By order of the Angel, Jonah captured Nineveh, Jonah had 3days interment in the belly of a fish. Habakkuk was lifted by an Angel to Babylon to provide Daniel with some food while he is in lion's den (Nah1:3;Rev14).

On that day the Lord will shield those who live in Jerusalem, so that the feeblest among them will be like David and the house of David like God like the Angel of the Lord going before them and the Lord came with his Angels from mountain Sinai, paran and seirt Zech12:8). Angels are mentioned 21 times in the book of Zechariah, in Judges 22 times and in Luke 23 times.

The angels of his power, presence, sanctification and guardian. The angels appeared throughout the book of Zechariah. Behold I will send my messenger (Mac. 3:1).

And the Angel of the Lord spoke unto Philip, saying arise and go toward the south unto the way that goeth down from Jerusalem unto Gaza, which is desert (Acts 8:6). For there stood by me this night Angel of God; whose I am and whose I serve (Acts27:23).

But the Angel of the Lord by night opened the prison door and brought them forth (Acts 5:19).

In (Heb 1:4) Angels were referred to as ministering spirits sent forth to minister for them who shall be hairs of salvation. In (Heb. 13:2) says be not forgetful to entertain Angels as strangers, thereby some entertain Angels unawares.

In the book of John 14:3, says He went to prepare a place before us.

God created Angels (Col 1:16). Angels were mentioned in Acts 23:18; 1Thi %:21; Psalm 33:6.

On the judgement day Children of the resurrection will be equal to the Angels, and will have wings. We are referred to as sons of God, not the Angels those who have the fear of God (Ps29:8; 73:15; Deut 32:5; 2Corinthians 5:17; Ex 6:6; Num 13:32; Job: 11:32; Matt 22; Luke24). Then the devil leaveth him and behold angels came and ministered unto him (Matt 4:11). An Angel of the Lord descended from Heaven and came and rolled away the stone (Matt28:2).

And the Angels which kept not their first Estate but left their own habitation he had reserved in everlasting chains under darkness unto the judgement of the great day (Jude 1:6). Yet Michael the archangel when contending with the devil, he disputed about the body of Moses durst not bring against him a railing accusation but said, the rebuke thee (Jude 1:9).

In (Rev.19:10) and I fell at his feet to worship and he said, see thou do it not for I am much fellow servant like you and thy brethren that have the testimony of Jesus Christ. Worship God for the Testimony of Jesus is the spirit of Prophesy. And I felt at his feet to worship and He said, see than do it not for I am much fellow servant and of thy brethren that have the testimony of Jesus Christ (Rev19:10).

Questions about Angels.

Do I have guardian Angel?

Possibly (Matt18:6-10; Acts12

Does God promise to protect us from all harm? No (2Cor12:7-10

Paul had to put up with weaknesses, insults, distresses, persecutions and difficulties. Note God does not promise absolute protection.

He said if we walk in His ways, He will protect us (Ps91:12).

If we keep sound wisdom and discretion, then we will be secured (Prov3:13, 21, 23). Remember Balaam left God's ways and his foot were dashed (Num22:25).

Does God promise to care for us? Yes: (Ps34:6-7; Matt6:26-33; ICor10:13; IPeter1:5). It was necessary for Jesus to be seen by Angels, so they could be His witnesses. Angels are afraid of accusing men to repent (2Peter2:10-12; Jude1:9). They do not dispense hope (Heb 11:1-6) they do not heal the sick (James 5:16).

Printed in the United States
By Bookmasters